LIBERTY UA. 19 AND A. 21: FINE LINE OF DISTINCTION

VOLUME 3, ISSUE 1 OF BRILLOPEDIA

KHUSHI KUMARI

Contents

Preface

"Start writing, no matter what. The water does not flow until the faucet is turned on".

• Louis L'Amour

Hundreds of students and professors are contributing their work to Brillopedia, we are here to provide ample information about Law and Contemporary issues. Our aim is to provide a platform for today's generation to express their views and ideas on law and contemporary law.

CHAPTER ONE

ABSTRACT

The Constitution of India through its Article 19 and 21 provides provision for protecting an individuals' liberty. The liberty listed in Article 19 is specific and general in nature, while the liberty mentioned in Article 21 has the word "personal" attached to it, implying that it refers to liberty of physical body and mind. The Judiciary in India has made an expansive interpretation of the word "personal liberty" under Article 21 and while doing so has ignored the word 'personal' and just focused on the word 'liberty' within it. As a result, a large number of rights have been created under its ambit whose reliability and delivery are subjective. Even though the expansive and liberal interpretation of Article was important to protect individuals' rights and interest, but doing so the judiciary has crossed its boundary and overused the provision.

This research paper aims at understanding and analyzing the fine line of difference between the 'liberty' mentioned under Article 19 and Article 21. While doing so, the paper tries to analyze the intention of framers of Constitution while adopting 'due process' concept and 'personal' before liberty under Article 21. Also, the paper includes certain rights which have been incorporated under the ambit of 'personal liberty' by the Indian judiciary and ends with a conclusive study for the same.

Keywords: Liberty, Personal Liberty, Rights, Judiciary, Constitution, Interpretation, Due process.

CHAPTER TWO

ENVISIONING INDIAN JUDICIARY

A Constituent Assembly was created before the independence of India for the future nation and a Drafting Committee was created for drafting Constitution, which had Dr. B.R. Ambedkar as its chairman. The Constitution of India has incorporated concepts from throughout the world, but it has not included them as it is, it has rather included them with some modifications.

The concept of establishment of the Supreme Court was borrowed from the United States of America, where the part of 'due process' was not adopted by the Indian framers as they believed that it needs to be modified. This was because the framers wanted to keep away from reading in of substantive rights, as they felt that the judiciary could use this part of the Constitutional provision to build obstacles in the path of legislature.[1]

I.1. Deliberation over 'due process' concept

The report on fundamental rights by the Advisory Committee on Minorities and Fundamental Rights presented Clause 9, now known as Article 21 of the Constitution as – *"No person shall be deprived of his life, or liberty, without due process of law, nor shall any person be denied the equal treatment of the laws within the territories of the Union: Provided that nothing herein contained shall detract from the powers of the Union Legislature in respect offoreigners"*.[2]

This clause was again amended by the Constituent Assembly as – *"No person shall be deprived of his life, or liberty, without due process of law, nor shall any person be denied equality before the law within the territories of the Union."*[3] After completion of the drafting, Article 21 was presented with *'personal'* being added before *'liberty'* and *'expect according to procedure established by law'* substituted in place of *'without due process of law'* in the

Clause 9.

I.2. Reasoning behind adopting *'procedure established by law'* concept

The reason behind putting *'personal'* before *'liberty'* was to prevent the rights protected by Article 19 to be granted to non-citizens too. The framers of constitution were of the opinion that the rights conferred under Article 19 and Article 21 should be treated separately. However, the reason behind choosing *'procedure established by law'* in place of *'due process of law'* was far more complex. The debate was generated at the time of the modification of the clause of *'due process of law'*, it was felt that this clause was not as specific and definite as *'procedure established by law'* which was borrowed from the Japanese Constitution. The major reason behind the change of *'due process'* concept was the nature of relationship between the judicial and the legislative part of the government. Two groups on the basis of opinion on the same can be created as –

a. **Wanted to adopt *'due process'* concept:**

Dr. B.R. Ambedkar – He was of the opinion that *'due process'* clause should be adopted as Judicial powers are required. He was also concerned about the procedural fairness and felt that Legislature are appointed by election and it can be extra arbitrary.

K.M. Munshi – It was pointed out by him that the clause of *'due process'* would only apply to liberty of person and not to liberty of contract as a result of addition of *'personal'* before *'liberty'* in Article 21.[4]

a. **Didn't wanted to adopt *'due process'* concept:**

B.N. Rau – He was the constitutional advisor to the Constituent Assembly and was concerned about substantive due process being abused by the Supreme Court of USA[5]. He pointed out that the clause of *'due process'* would get into the way of social legislation which is beneficial. When B.N. Rau met Justice Felix Frankfurter, Justice Felix persuaded him into thinking and believing that *'due process'* confers the power of judicial review, which is could result into becoming burden for judiciary and was undemocratic.[6] Also, according to him, if Judiciary is given this power, it will cut short the legislative jurisdiction.

At last, B.N. Rau was successful in convincing the Drafting Committee to omit the due process clause.

Another reason for the same was the communal violence which the nation was facing after its partition. It was believed that communal violence could be better checked without the constitutional guarantees of due process in the preventive detention policies, which were used during the rule of Britishers.

I.3. Result of the changes:

To bring a *"social revolution, of national renascence"* was the ultimate goal which was to be served by the Constitution.[7] And this goal was supposed to be fulfilled by executive and legislature rather than the judiciary. The judiciary was not expected to become "super-executive or super-legislature". Therefore, it can be said that the Judiciary in India was not designed as some strong institution which could challenge laws on the ground of substantive due process.[8] By using 'procedure established by law' clause the framers of the Constitution wanted to prevent the judiciary from giving more importance to rights of the individuals rather than beneficial social legislations.

The right under Article 14, 19 and 21 were strictly separated by the framers for the above-mentioned reasons by using 'reasonable restrictions' in the language of Article 19. It was envisioned that no link between the said articles can be formed as they confer separate rights. Also, it would not be possible for the judiciary to increase and extend the concept of judicial review to Article 21 from Article 19.[9] The reasonable of the provisions which deprived a person from his or her life and liberty were not supposed to be looked into by the judges, whereas in case where a person is deprived of his or her right of movement or expression, reasonableness of such provisions can be checked. This was so as to prevent *'due process'* clause to enter into the system in India.[10]

[1] See generally 7, CONSTITUENT ASSEMB. DEB. (Dec. 6 and 13, 1948).

[2]Shivangi Gangwar, *'Due Process' v. 'Procedure Established by Law' Framing and Working the Indian Constitution*, 1.3 CALQ (2013) 15, Supreme Court Cases, 18-19 (2013).

[3]3, CONSTITUENT ASSEMB. DEB. (Apr. 30, 1947), available at http://parliamentofindia.nic.in/ls/debates/vol3p3.htm (Accessed on April 25, 2021)

[4]GRANVILLE AUSTIN, THE INDIAN CONSTITUTION, 105 (1966).

[5] DURGA DAS BASU, SHORTER CONSTITUTION OF INDIA, 693 (13th ed. 2001).

[6]Shivangi Gangwar, *'Due Process' v. 'Procedure Established by Law' Framing and Working the Indian Constitution,* 1.3 CALQ (2013) 15, Supreme Court Cases, 20 (2013).

[7] GRANVILLE AUSTIN, THE INDIAN CONSTITUTION, 27 (1966).

[8]Shivangi Gangwar, *'Due Process' v. 'Procedure Established by Law' Framing and Working the Indian Constitution,* 1.3 CALQ (2013) 15, Supreme Court Cases, 21 (2013).

[9] Charles Henry Alexandrowicz-Alexander, American Influence on Constitutional Interpretation in India, 5 AM. J. COMP. L. 98, 100 (1956).

[10]Shivangi Gangwar, *'Due Process' v. 'Procedure Established by Law' Framing and Working the Indian Constitution,* 1.3 CALQ (2013) 15, Supreme Court Cases, 21 (2013).

CHAPTER THREE

II. 'LIBERTY' U/A. 19 OF THE CONSTITUTION

The right to liberty has been guaranteed to all the citizens by the virtue of Article 19 of the Constitution. Without liberty, there is no democracy and the liberty under Article 19 is closely linked to the preamble's goal of "sovereign democratic republic".[1] Article 19 is different from other provisions in the constitution which mentions liberty as they talk about 'personal liberty' whereas Article 19 is concerned with basic 'liberty'. It has been included in the constitution to secure individuals' liberty and therefore it forms the heart of freedom.[2] Many aspects of liberty are covered under Article 19 which states that – *"all citizens shall have the right:*

a. *to freedom of speech and expression;*
b. *to assemble peaceably and without arms;*
c. *to form association and unions;*
d. *to move freely throughout the territory of India;*
e. *to reside and settle in any part of India;*
f. *****
g. *to practice any profession or to carry on any occupation, trade or business."*[3]

The rights mentioned herein are not absolute in nature, they are rather limited with reasonable restrictions. It was stated by the court in the case of *Gopalan vs State of Madras* (1950) that "there cannot be any such thing as absolute or uncontrolled liberty wholly freed from restraint, for that would lead to anarchy and disorder". The reasonable restrictions are mentioned from Article 19(2) to Article 19(6). The purpose of these restrictions is to regulate freedom of an individual and promote society's greater interest.

Also, the Supreme Court has opined that "For the Constitution, therefore, what the state attempts to do in declaring the rights is to strike a balance between individual liberty and social security".[4]

[1]Nirmalendu Bikash Rakshit, *Mutilated Liberty and the Constitution*, 38 EPW 1548, 1548 (2003).

[2]DD BASU, INTRODUCTION TO THE CONSTITUTION OF INDIA 39 (2011).

[3]INDIA CONSTI. art. 19.

[4]Nirmalendu Bikash Rakshit, *Mutilated Liberty and the Constitution*, 38 EPW 1548, 1548 (2003).

CHAPTER FOUR

'PERSONAL LIBERTY' U/A. 21 OF THE CONSTITUTION

"Protection of life and personal liberty - No person shall be deprived of his life or personal liberty except according to procedure established by law."[1]

It can be understood by the Constituent Assembly Debates that they had no intention to introduce American doctrine in the Indian context. But the substantive due process jurisprudence was found by the Supreme Court anyhow within the area of the Constitution, which on the other hand intended to exclude it.

The meaning and scope of the term "personal liberty" has kept changing since the enforcement of Constitution by virtue of different judicial pronouncements. Initially, the meaning of "personal liberty" emerged from the Supreme Court's consideration in the case of *A.K. Gopalan v. State of Madras*[2] but it was then overruled by the Supreme Court in the case of *Maneka Gandhi v. Union of India*[3] and then the scope was widened. Therefore, the same has been discussed in two parts – first, the *A.K. Gopalan* Phase and second, the *Maneka Gandhi* Phase.

1. The *A.K. Gopalan* Phase

Article 21 was discussed in the case of **A.K. Gopalan v. State of Madras**[4], which was one of the initial cases to do so. In this case, Gopalan was detained under the Preventive Detention Act of 1950 which was then challenged by him on the ground that it violates his rights under Article 13, 19, 21 and 22. Gopalan claimed that freedoms guaranteed under Article 19 are also included under the 'personal liberty'. This argument was not accepted by the majority whose decision was authored by Chief Justice Kania, he said that Article 21 and Article 19 should not be read together. The reason behind him saying that was that Article 19 deals with substantive rights whereas Article 21 deals with procedural rights and the 'procedure established by law' under Article 21 did not mean 'due process of law'. Therefore, the laws dealing with preventive detention could not be seen through the lens of Article 19.

The Supreme Court in this case considered the rights conferred under Article 14, 19 and 21 as mutually exclusive one. The Constituent Assembly debate was referred by Justice Mukherjea, who opined that the intention of the framers to put 'personal' before liberty under Article 21 was to exclude its contents from Article 19. The power of final determination of laws was given to the legislature by the Constitution and therefore, Chief Justice Kania arrived at this narrow interpretation of Article 19 and limited the scope of judicial function, apparently using both tools of original intent and textual analysis.[5][6] Justice Fazl Ali was the only one who had dissenting opinion in this case, he opined that right guaranteed under Article 19(1)(d) was being violated by the preventive detention. And according to him, preventive detention laws would be subject to the limited judicial review even by a narrow construction of this provision.[7] To conclude, the Supreme Court in this case held that "personal liberty" under Article 21 of the Constitution merely means liberty of the physical body i.e. freedom from detention and arrest without the authority of law and nothing more than that.[8]

The beginning of right to privacy was marked in the case of ***Kharak Singh v. State of Uttar Pradesh*[9]**, in which Uttar Pradesh Police Regulation 236 was challenged on the ground that it violates Article 19(1)(d) and Article 21 as it allowed police surveillance and night domiciliary visits of house of a suspect. The decision of the majority was that as the impugned regulation was open to challenge as a result of it not being passed under the authority of any law. The court held that the provision of Regulation 236 which dealt with domiciliary visits are violative of Article 21 and therefore, held it unconstitutional. Also, it held that the rights which are not covered under Article 19 should be included under Article 21. Justice Subba Rao, who had the dissenting opinion said that Article 19 and Article 21 have a considerable overlap even though they both dealt with different fundamental rights. He also was of the opinion that right to privacy is a part of Article 21 as it is an important ingredient of 'personal liberty' and therefore, it has to be shown by the impugned regulation that it does not infringe rights under both Article 19 and Article 21.

2. The *Maneka Gandhi* Phase

The case of **Maneka Gandhi v. Union of India**[10]was a turning point of the jurisprudence of substantive due process rights. It was the first case after the Emergency period to deal with "personal liberty". The petitioner in this case on her passport getting impounded by the Janata government, challenged such order on the ground that it violated her Article 14 and 21. This was so because she was not provided any prior notice or hearing. The majority decision of the court expanded the scope of "personal liberty" under Article 21 and included within its ambit the right to travel abroad. The Supreme Court in this case overruled the decision in the *Gopalan* case and held that the procedure followed by Article 21 should be fair and just and it should not be oppressive, fanciful or arbitrary, which are the principles of natural justice. The court in this case said that the term "personal liberty" under Article 21 of the Constitution should be interpreted in the widest sense possible. Also, "it covers a variety of rights which go to constitute the personal liberty of man and some of them have raised the status of distinct fundamental rights and given additional protection under Article 19."[11]

In the case of **Icchu Devi Choraria v. Union of India**[12], the wordings of the court were as follows:

3. ... *"The courts should always lean in favour of upholding personal liberty, for it is one of the most cherished values of mankind. Without it life would not be worth living. It is one of the pillars of free democratic society. Men have rightly laid down their lives at its altar in order to secure it, protect it and preserve it. The Constitution has therefore, while conceding the power of preventive detention, provided procedural safeguards with a view to protecting the citizen against arbitrary and unjustified invasion of personal liberty and the courts have always zealously tried to uphold and enforce these safeguards. This Court has also through its judicial pronouncements created various legal bulwarks and breakwaters into the vast powers conferred on the executive by the laws of preventive detention prevalent at different points of time."*

5. ...*"Article 21 of the Constitution provides in clear and explicit terms that no one shall be derived of his life or personal liberty except in accordance with procedure established by law. The constitutional right of life and personal liberty is placed on such a high pedestal by this Court that it has always insisted that whenever there is any deprivation of life or personal liberty, the authority responsible for such deprivation must satisfy the court that it has acted in accordance with the law. This is an area where the court had been most strict and scrupulous in ensuring observance with the requirements of the law, and*

even where a requirement of the law is breached in the slightest measure, the court has not hesitated to strike down the order of detention...The court has always regarded personal liberty as the most precious possession of mankind and refused to tolerate illegal detention, regardless of the social cost involved in the release of a possible renegade."

Going further in the case of ***Kartar Singh v. State of Punjab***[13], the Apex Court said that the root of Article 21 lies into the personal liberty provided within it and each expression used in the provision promotes in increasing the dignity and values of a human.

After the expansive interpretation of 'personal liberty' under Article 21, this liberty has been given the dimension of liberty of physical body and liberty of mind. And in reference to this, plethora of rights have been created by the judiciary.

[1]INDIA CONSTI. art. 21.

[2]*A.K. Gopalan v. State of Madras*, AIR 1950 SC 2 (India).

[3]*Maneka Gandhi v. Union of India*, (1978) 1 SCC 248 (India).

[4]*A.K. Gopalan v. State of Madras*, AIR 1950 SC 2 (India).

[5] Manoj Mate, *The Origins of Due Process in India : The Role of Borrowing in Personal Liberty and Preventive Detention Cases*, 28 Berkeley J. Int'l L. 216, 232 (2010).

[6]Shivangi Gangwar, *'Due Process' v. 'Procedure Established by Law' Framing and Working the Indian Constitution*, 1.3 CALQ (2013) 15, Supreme Court Cases, 25-26 (2013).

[7]Shivangi Gangwar, *'Due Process' v. 'Procedure Established by Law' Framing and Working the Indian Constitution*, 1.3 CALQ (2013) 15, Supreme Court Cases, 25-26 (2013).

[8]Devendra Kumar Arora, *Harmonising Liberty and Security in Social Order*, (2013) 7 SCC (J).

[9]*Kharak Singh v. State of Uttar Pradesh*, 1964 S.C.R. (1) 332 (India).

[10]*Maneka Gandhi v. Union of India*, (1978) 1 SCC 248 (India).

[11]*Maneka Gandhi v. Union of India*, (1978) 1 SCC 248 (India).

[12]*Icchu Devi Choraria v. Union of India*, (1980) 4 SCC 531 (India).

[13]*Kartar Singh v. State of Punjab*, (1994) 3 SCC 569 (India).

CHAPTER FIVE

INFERENCE

It was not intended by the framers of the Constitution that the judiciary would become "super-executive or super-legislative." As a result, it can be said that the Indian judiciary was not intended to be a powerful institution capable of overturning laws on the basis of substantive due process. The framers of the Constitution aimed to prevent the judiciary from prioritizing individual rights over beneficial social legislations by using the "procedure defined by statute" clause. The framers used the phrase "reasonable restrictions" in the language of Article 19 and "personal liberty" in the language of Article 21 to clearly distinguish the rights under Articles 19 and 21.Since the articles grant different rights, it was assumed that no relation could be established between them. However, the Supreme Court considers substantive due process jurisprudence to be within the scope of the Constitution.

From *A.K. Gopalan's* rigid construction of "Personal Liberty" to the Supreme Court's expansion of the horizon in respect of the word "life" to include all the requisite rights, to make life "effective, meaningful, and worth living," Article 21 has undergone a turbulent "Revolution."After the Supreme Court's decision in *A.K. Gopalan*, the protection given under Article 21 was limited to the freedom of the individual against unlawful restraint. But in the case of *Maneka Gandhi,* not only the decision of *A.K. Gopalan* was overruled but also the scope of "personal liberty" was significantly widened. It is clear that the distinction between life and personal liberty has vanished, and that the majority of the rights enumerated under the term "life" are merely liberties, and that the two expressions have merged to a large extent.

Even though expansive interpretation of Article 21 was needed, it was still not meant to be filled with rights, which was created by the judiciary. It can be said that the "personal liberty" under Article 21 has been overused by the judiciary as a plethora of rights have been created and incorporated under the ambit of Article 21. Rights like Right to Shelter which has been included under the ambit of Article 21 by the judiciary is subjective in nature because of the question which arises on its delivery. Many questions can also be raised on the reliability of rights like in case of physical cruelty which is a ground of divorce under the Hindu Marriage Act of 1955, the evidence for the same can be relied on. Bur when it comes to mental cruelty, which has been included as a ground for divorce under the said act by the 1976 amendment, the evidence of the same cannot be fully relied upon.

The separation of power which was created by the Constitution framers are not adhered by the judiciary, who is on the run to become a super legislature. Due to the plethora of rights created by the judiciary under Article 21, the claims under the same are increasing with a huge pace. The judiciary has ignored the "personal" word attached before "liberty" under Article 21 and is just focusing on the word "liberty" in it. And therefore, has lost the fine line of distinction that was made by the framers of constitution between 'liberty' under Article 19 and Article 21.